Pete's
NEW
SHOES

Pete needed some new shoes.
Mom took him to the shoe store.

2

Pete tried on some brown shoes.
"They're too tight!" said Pete.

4

He tried on some black shoes.
"They're too big!" said Pete.

6

He tried on some shoes with buckles.
"I can't do up buckles!" said Pete.

8

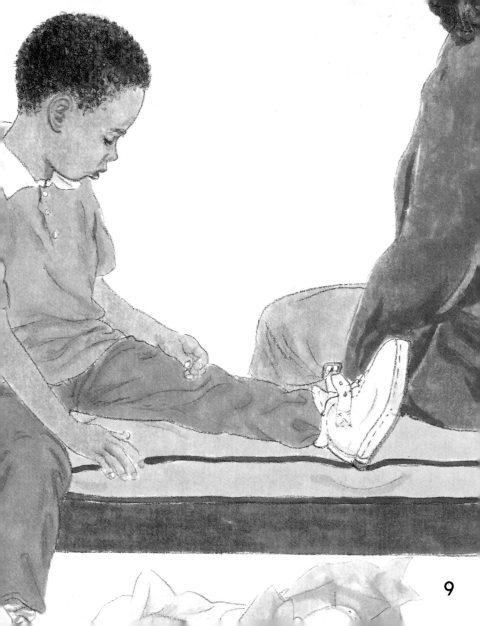

He tried on some shoes with laces.
"I can't do up laces!" said Pete.

He tried on some shoes
with straps.
The straps stuck together
by themselves.

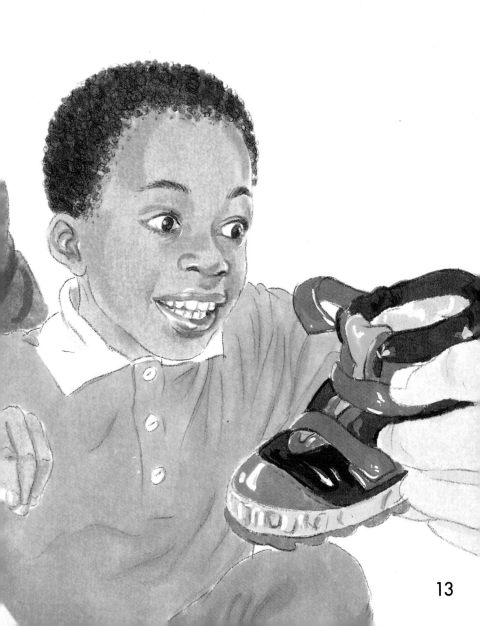

"I like these shoes!" said Pete.
"They are just right for me."

"Thank goodness!" said Mom.

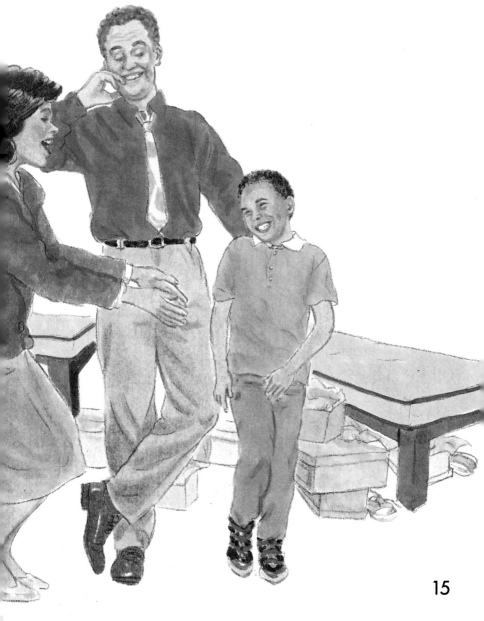